FOCUS

on Spelling

D0620051

Spelling

Book 3

**Joyce Sweeney and
Carol Doncaster**

FOCUS
on Spelling

Using this book

This book will help you to develop good spelling strategies that you can use in your writing.

What's in a unit

Each unit is set out in the same way as the example here.

Unit heading — This tells you what you will be learning about.

Focus — This helps you think about the spelling rule.

More to think about — Activities to practise and develop your understanding.

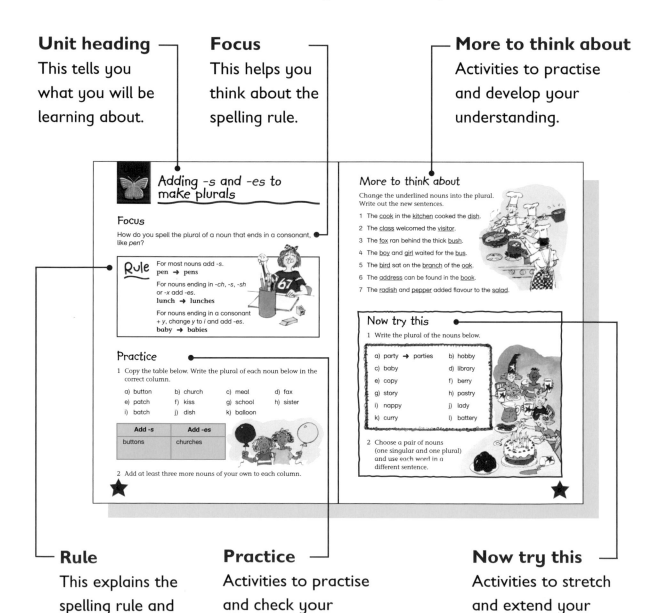

Adding -s and -es to make plurals

Focus

How do you spell the plural of a noun that ends in a consonant, like *pen*?

Rule
For most nouns add -s.
pen ➔ pens

For nouns ending in -ch, -s, -sh or -x add -es.
lunch ➔ lunches

For nouns ending in a consonant + y, change y to i and add -es.
baby ➔ babies

Practice

1 Copy the table below. Write the plural of each noun below in the correct column.

a) button   b) church   c) meal   d) fax
e) patch   f) kiss   g) school h) sister
i) batch   j) dish   k) balloon

Add -s	Add -es
buttons	churches

2 Add at least three more nouns of your own to each column.

More to think about

Change the underlined nouns into the plural. Write out the new sentences.

1 The <u>cook</u> in the <u>kitchen</u> cooked the <u>dish</u>.
2 The <u>class</u> welcomed the <u>visitor</u>.
3 The <u>fox</u> ran behind the thick <u>bush</u>.
4 The <u>boy</u> and <u>girl</u> waited for the <u>bus</u>.
5 The <u>bird</u> sat on the <u>branch</u> of the <u>oak</u>.
6 The <u>address</u> can be found in the <u>book</u>.
7 The <u>radish</u> and <u>pepper</u> added flavour to the <u>salad</u>.

Now try this

1 Write the plural of the nouns below.

a) party ➔ parties   b) hobby
c) baby   d) library
e) copy   f) berry
g) story   h) pastry
i) nappy   j) lady
k) curry   l) battery

2 Choose a pair of nouns (one singular and one plural) and use each word in a different sentence.

Rule — This explains the spelling rule and gives examples.

Practice — Activities to practise and check your understanding.

Now try this — Activities to stretch and extend your understanding.

Contents

Adding -s and -es to make plurals

Focus

How do you spell the plural of a noun that ends in a consonant, like *pen*?

Rule

For most nouns add -s.
pen → **pens**

For nouns ending in -*ch*, -*s*, -*sh* or -*x* add -*es*.
lunch → **lunches**

For nouns ending in a consonant + *y*, change *y* to *i* and add -*es*.
baby → **babies**

Practice

1 Copy the table below. Write the plural of each noun below in the correct column.

a) button   b) church   c) meal   d) fax

e) patch   f) kiss   g) school   h) sister

i) batch   j) dish   k) balloon

Add -*s*	Add -*es*
buttons	churches

2 Add at least three more nouns of your own to each column.

More to think about

Change the underlined nouns into the plural.
Write out the new sentences.

1 The <u>cook</u> in the <u>kitchen</u> cooked the <u>dish</u>.

2 The <u>class</u> welcomed the <u>visitor</u>.

3 The <u>fox</u> ran behind the thick <u>bush</u>.

4 The <u>boy</u> and <u>girl</u> waited for the <u>bus</u>.

5 The <u>bird</u> sat on the <u>branch</u> of the <u>oak</u>.

6 The <u>address</u> can be found in the <u>book</u>.

7 The <u>radish</u> and <u>pepper</u> added flavour to the <u>salad</u>.

Now try this

1 Write the plural of the nouns below.

a) party ➔ parties   b) hobby

c) baby   d) library

e) copy   f) berry

g) story   h) pastry

i) nappy   j) lady

k) curry   l) battery

2 Choose a pair of nouns
(one singular and one plural)
and use each word in a
different sentence.

5

Other plurals

Focus

How do you spell the plural of a noun that ends in *–f* or *–fe*, like *elf* or *wife*?

 Rule   For most words that end in *-f*, change the *f* to *v* and add *-es*.
elf ➜ **elves**

For most words that end in *-fe*, drop the *fe* and add *-ves*.
wife ➜ **wives**

Some nouns have unusual plurals and need to be learned by heart.
ox ➜ **oxen**
mouse ➜ **mice**
goose ➜ **geese**

Practice

1 Write each word and its plural.

a) scarf ➜ scarves   b) self   c) thief   d) half

e) wolf   f) knife   g) loaf   h) life   i) calf

2 The word below *does not* end in *-f* or *-fe* in the singular. Write the word and its singular form.

gloves ➜ _____

More to think about

Copy the table. Write the plurals of the nouns in the correct column.

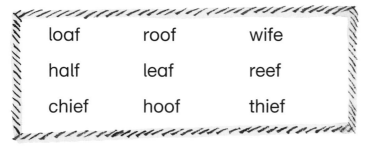

loaf	roof	wife
half	leaf	reef
chief	hoof	thief

Nouns that follow the rule	Nouns that do not follow the rule
loaves	roofs

Now try this

Some nouns have unusual plurals. Copy the table. Write the singular and the plural nouns in the correct column.

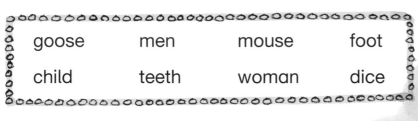

| goose | men | mouse | foot |
| child | teeth | woman | dice |

Singular	Plural
goose	geese

Plurals of nouns ending in vowels

Focus

How do you spell the plural of a noun that ends in a vowel other than *e*, like *sofa* or *tomato*?

Rule For most nouns ending in vowels other than -*e*, add -*s* to make the plural.
sofa + s = sofas

Some nouns ending in -*o* add -*es* to make the plural.
tomato ➜ tomatoes

Practice

Write the nouns.

1
banjos

2

3

4

5

6

7

8

9

More to think about

Plurals of some nouns ending in *-o* add *-es*.
Work out the clues, then write the words and their plurals.

1   a person who has done something
brave or good   h<u>ero</u>   →   h<u>eroes</u>

2   a wild animal like a large cow, with
long curved horns   b_____ → _____

3   a white vegetable that has a brown
or red skin and grows underground   p_____ → _____

4   a mountain with an opening at the
top from which lava sometimes erupts   v_____ → _____

5   the repeat of a sound caused by the
sound being bounced back off a surface   e_____ → _____

6   a small, round, red fruit used as
a vegetable   t_____ → _____

7   a violent storm with strong circular winds
around a funnel-shaped cloud   t_____ → _____

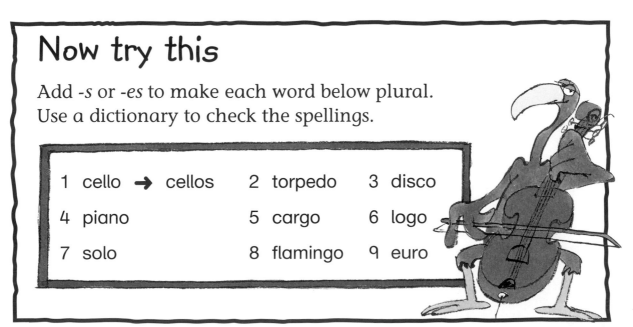

Now try this

Add *-s* or *-es* to make each word below plural.
Use a dictionary to check the spellings.

1 cello → cellos	2 torpedo	3 disco
4 piano	5 cargo	6 logo
7 solo	8 flamingo	9 euro

The prefixes auto-, bi-, over-, sub-, tele- and trans-

Focus

What is a prefix? What does it do? Let's look at the prefixes *auto-*, *bi-*, *over-*, *sub-*, *tele-* and *trans-*.

> **Rule** A prefix is a group of letters at the beginning of a word that can help you to work out the meaning of a word.
> *auto-* means "self"
> *bi-* means "two" or "twice"
> *over-* means "too much"
> *sub-* means "under" or "below"
> *tele-* means "distant"
> *trans-* means "across"
>
> An ***over**loaded* truck has too big a load.
> A ***bi**cycle* has two wheels.

Practice

Add a prefix to each word to make a new word. You can use some prefixes more than once.

| auto- | bi- | tele- | trans- | sub- | over- |

1 phone ➜ telephone
2 vision
3 focal
4 port
5 way
6 atlantic
7 scope
8 graph
9 plant
10 crowd

10

More to think about

1 Write a definition for each word below.
   Use a dictionary to help you.

   a) overweight b) overflow

   c) bilingual d) bisect

   e) teletext f) telecommunications

   g) translate h) transfer

2 Now choose four words from question 1
   and use each word in a sentence.

Now try this

Use the clues to work out the words. Each word starts with a
different prefix. Write the words. Use a dictionary to check
the spellings.

| auto- | bi- | tele- | trans- | sub- | over- |

1 an account of someone's life that they
   have written themselves
   autobiography

2 a person who uses two languages is this

3 a place thickly covered with plants and
   weeds is this

4 a type of ship that can travel beneath
   the surface of the sea

5 an operation where an organ is taken
   from one person and put into another

6 when you become 100 years old you
   receive one of these from the Queen

11

The prefixes fore-, kilo-, inter- and mini-

Focus

Let's look at the prefixes *fore-*, *kilo-*, *inter-* and *mini-*.

Rule

fore-	means "before" in time or "at or near the front"
kilo-	means "a thousand"
inter-	means "between"
mini-	means "smaller" or "less important"

Practice

1 Add a prefix to each word to make a new word. You can use some prefixes more than once.

fore-	kilo-	inter-	mini-

a) cast → forecast   b) gram

c) metre   d) national

e) bus   f) view

g) ground   h) beast

i) name   j) head

2 *Inter* means "between". Use this information to work out the meanings of these words.

a) interactive   b) intercom   c) intermediate

Use a dictionary to check your answers. Write the words and the dictionary definitions.

More to think about

1 Write the words and underline the prefix. Then write a definition for each word, using your dictionary to help you.

a) <u>inter</u>net   b) foreground

c) forehead   d) intersect

e) miniskirt   f) kilometre

2 Now choose three words from question 1, each beginning with a different prefix. Use each word in a sentence.

Now try this

1 Write each word and underline the prefix each time.

a) triangle ➜ <u>tri</u>angle   b) tricycle   c) tripod

What does the prefix mean?
Now use each word in a sentence.

2 Write a definition for each word below. Check the meaning in your dictionary.

a) triplets   b) triple   c) trio

13

Word families

Focus

What is a word family? How can it help you to spell?

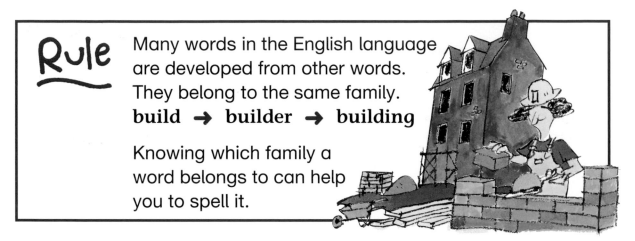

Rule Many words in the English language are developed from other words. They belong to the same family.

build → builder → building

Knowing which family a word belongs to can help you to spell it.

Practice

The words below can be sorted into word families. Write the words in the correct columns.

package	passenger	relation
actor	activity	packet
action	packing	passable
passage	related	relative

relate	**pass**	**pack**	**act**
related			

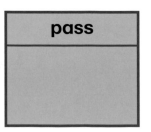 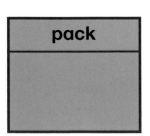 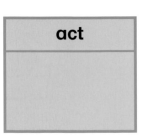

More to think about

1 *To observe* means "to watch something carefully".
The definitions below are all for words which have developed
from the word *observe*. Use the clues to work out the words.

   a) someone who notices things that are not usually noticed is this

   b) a room or building containing telescopes for studying the sun,
moon, planets and stars

   c) a person who watches rather than takes part

2 To direct someone somewhere means
"to tell them how to get there".
The definitions below are all for words
which have developed from the word *direct*.
Use the clues to work out the words.

   a) a person who decides how a film or
play is made or performed

   b) a book that gives lists of information such
as names, addresses and telephone numbers

   c) instructions that tell you how to get somewhere

Now try this

Find at least two words that belong to each word family.
Write them in the correct column.

music	hair	sign
musician		

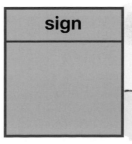

The suffixes -ful and -fully

Focus

What is a suffix? What does it do? Let's look at the suffixes -ful and -fully.

Rule A suffix is a group of letters added at the end of a word.

For most words, just add *-ful* or *-fully*.

tear ➜ **tearful** ➜ **tearfully**

For words ending in a consonant + *y*, change the *y* to *i* then add *-ful* or *-fully*.

beauty ➜ **beautiful** ➜ **beautifully**

Practice

Copy and complete the table using the words in the box below.

Word	Add *-ful*	Add *-fully*
play	playful	playfully

1 peace	2 pity	3 wonder	4 fear
5 mourn	6 duty	7 delight	8 plenty
9 power	10 cheer	11 faith	12 truth

More to think about

Choose a word from the box to complete the phrases.

| disgraceful | dutiful | powerful | tearful |

1
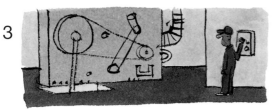
a _____ mess

2

a _____ farewell

3

a _____ machine

4

a _____ daughter

Now try this

Add *-ful* or *-fully* to the root word to complete the sentences.

1 It is <u>doubtful</u> that the match will take place.   doubt

2 Letters can be signed "Yours _____".   faith

3 The _____ puppy chewed the slippers.   play

4 The nurse _____ removed the glass from the wound.   care

5 Mr James is becoming very _____.   forget

Progress test 1

A Write the words.

1

d_____

2
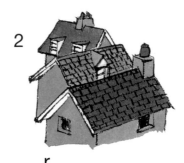
r_____

3

t_____

4

s_____

5

w_____

6

b_____

B Add a prefix to complete the words.

1

____cycle

2

____graph

3

____phone

4

____port

5

____marine

6

____flow

18

C Copy the table. Circle the words that belong to the same word family.

vary	→	varnish	(variety)	(various)	
secret	→	secrecy	secretive	secure	
miser	→	mischief	miserable	misery	
occupy	→	occupation	occasion	occupant	
hero	→	heroic	heroine	heron	
music	→	musical	musician	museum	

D

| doubtful | | harmful | | peaceful |

| awful | | wrongful | | dreadful |

Use the words above to complete the sentences.

1 It is _____ if they will come again after the _____ journey.

2 A _____ arrest was made at the _____ demonstration.

3 The _____ substance had an _____ smell.

Well done – you've finished your progress test.

19

The suffix -ing

Focus

What happens when you add the suffix *-ing* to a word?

Rule

When a word has a short vowel sound and one consonant, *double* the last consonant before adding *-ing*.

rub ➜ **rubbing**

When a word has a long vowel sound, do *not* double the last consonant.

rain ➜ **raining**

When a word has two consonants after a short vowel sound, do *not* double the last consonant.

send ➜ **sending**

When the root word ends in *-e*, drop the *e* before adding *-ing*.

hide ➜ **hiding**

Practice

1 Copy the table below. Write each word in the correct column.

dream	creep	snap	flit
swim	train	jog	break

Long vowel	Short vowel
dream	snap

2 Now add *-ing* to each word.

More to think about

1 The words below all have a short vowel sound.
  Add -*ing* to the words.

wrap ➡ wrapping	lift	bend
clap	hit	rust
chop	win	slip
dust	chat	melt

2 Now sort the -*ing* words from question 1 into two types by
  completing the table. Write a heading for each column.

wrapping	lifting

3 These words have a long vowel sound. Add -*ing* to these words.

ride	slope	write	blame	tune

Now try this

The -*ing* words in the sentences below have been spelled
wrongly. Write the sentences correctly.

1 The joiner is fiting a new lock on the window.
   The joiner is fitting a new lock on the window.

2 We went skatting on the frozen pond.

3 I am hopping to win the hoping race.

4 The man is moping the sticky floor.

5 The dog was chaseing the cat.

21

Soft c

Focus

How do you spell words with the soft *c* sound, like *century*?

Rule	The letter *c* makes the sound "*s*" when it is followed by *e*, *i* or *y*. **century** **decide** **cymbals**

Practice

1 Write the words and circle the soft *c* sound in each word.

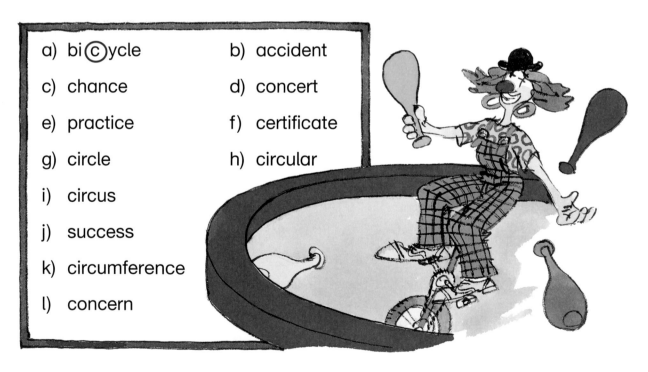

a) bi ⓒ ycle   b) accident

c) chance   d) concert

e) practice   f) certificate

g) circle   h) circular

i) circus

j) success

k) circumference

l) concern

2 Now choose three words from those above and use each word in a sentence.

More to think about

Soft *c* has been missed out in the words below. Write the words, putting the letter *c* in the correct place. Circle the *c* in each word, like this:

elery ➜ (c)elery   stenil ➜ sten(c)il

1 ymbals	2 deimal	3 exept
4 inema	5 reent	6 entury
7 groer	8 ell	9 deide
10 ity	11 ereal	12 Deember

Now try this

New words can be made from one word by changing the onset (the first sound).
In the word *price*, *pr* is the onset.

    pr + **ice** = **price**
  onset

1 Change the onset to make new words.
   Write at least four new rhyming words in each box.

face
place

price

2 Now use one set of rhyming words to write a short poem.

Soft g

Focus

How do you spell words with the soft *g* sound, like *magic*?

 Soft *g* sounds like *j* as in *jug*.
Soft *g* is usually spelled with a *g* before *e*, *i* or *y*.
germ

A soft *g* sound is usually spelled with a *g* when it comes in the middle of a word.
magic

A soft *g* sound is usually spelled *-ge* when it comes at the end of a word.
cage

Practice

Copy and complete the table, using the words below.

giant	garden	giraffe	gentle
goose	gym	garlic	golf
general	ginger	gobble	genius
goldfish	gallop	gardener	gerbil

Soft *g*	Hard *g*
giant	garden

24

More to think about

1 Write the words.

2 Read the clues and write the words.

a) someone you have never met before

str_____

b) an event or situation that is disastrous or very sad

tr_____

c) a largish bird with grey feathers, often seen in towns

p_____

d) a moveable joint that attaches a door or window to its frame

h_____

e) a boat with a flat bottom, used for carrying heavy loads

b_____

Now try this

Rhyming can help you to spell. Write four rhyming words in each column.

cage	nudge
rage	

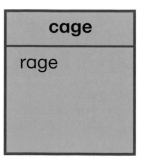  

The letter strings ear, ight and ough

Focus

Did you know that the same letters can make different sounds? Let's look at the letter strings *ear*, *ight* and *ough*.

 Rule

The letter string *ear* can have different pronunciations:
ear as in **bear**d
air as in p**ear**
er as in **ear**th
ar as in h**ear**t

The letter string *ight* can sound like *ite*.
n**ight**

When the letter *e* comes before *ight*, the letter string can sound like *ate*.
we**ight**

Practice

1 Add the letter string *ear* to complete the words below.

a) d<u>ear</u>

b) b_____

c) s_____ch

d) cl_____

e) _____ n

f) n_____

g) l_____n

h) f_____

i) sp_____

j) g_____

k) w_____

l) h_____d

2 Copy and complete the table using the words from question 1.

Sounds like *pear*	Sounds like *beard*	Sounds like *earth*
	dear	

More to think about

1 Add *ight* or *eight* to complete the words.

a) r<u>ight</u>　　　　b) w<u>eight</u>

c) f_____　　　　　d) br_____

e) fr_____　　　　　f) l_____

2 Copy and complete the table using the words from question 1.

Sounds like *kite*	Sounds like *ate*

Now try this

The letter string *ough* can represent different sounds.

I take it you already know
of tough and bough and cough and dough?
Others may stumble but not you,
On hiccough, thorough, laugh and through.
Well done! And now you wish, perhaps,
To learn of more familiar traps.

Extract from a letter published in the *London Times* (3 January 1965)

1 Write the words in the poem that have the same letter string but different pronunciations.

2 These *ough* words sound like four *ough* words in the poem. Write each word and the word it sounds like from the poem.

trough　　rough　　though　　borough

27

A Write the words. Each contains a soft _c_ sound.

1

2

3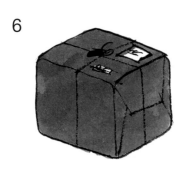

4

5

6

B Write the words. Each contains a soft _g_ sound.

1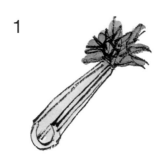

2

3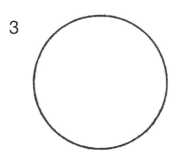

4

5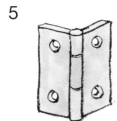

6

C Write the words.

1

h_____

2

d_____

3

b_____

4

r_____

5

fr_____

6

c_____

D Write the correct word.

1

pale/pail

2

chute/shoot

3

seller/cellar

4

flour/flower

5

heel/heal

6

breaks/brakes

Well done – you've finished your progress test.

29

Homophones

Focus

Did you know that some words sound the same but have different spellings, like *by* and *buy*?

 Rule Words that sound the same but have different spellings are called homophones.

Nusrin waved *goodbye* as she went *by* bus to *buy* some shoes.

Practice

Write a definition for each word. Use a dictionary to help you.

Word	Definition
waste	rubbish that is no longer wanted
waist	the middle part of your body where it narrows slightly above your hips
grate	
great	
sell	
cell	
hole	
whole	

More to think about

1 Choose the correct homophone to complete the sentence.

peace	bored	plane	piece	plain	board

a) Here is a large _____ of cake.

b) At last, there was _____ and quiet.

c) The wheel on the skate_____ was broken.

d) Darren was _____ with the wedding speeches.

e) The pastry chef used _____ flour.

f) The _____ made an emergency landing.

2 There are four more words in the sentences
above which have homophones. The words
begin with *h*, *t*, *f* and *m*. Write the words and
their homophones. For example:

here + hear

Now try this

Find two homophones for the words in the
first column. Copy and complete the table.

by	buy	bye
to		
so		
rain		
road		
sent		

Possessive pronouns

Focus

What are possessive pronouns? How are they used?

> ### Rule
> Possessive pronouns can be used instead of people's names. They tell us who things belong to.
>
> **That is the Smiths' house.** **The house is *theirs*.**
> **This is Mary's coat.** **The coat is *hers*.**

Practice

Use a possessive pronoun to complete the sentence.
Use each pronoun once only.

ours	hers	his	theirs	mine

1 The book is __hers__ .

2 The bikes are _____.

3 The shoe is _____.

4 The helmet is _____.

5 The computer is ____.

More to think about

1 Complete the sentences with a possessive pronoun.

a) This is Nicole's hat. This hat is _____.

b) This is Abdul's bike. This bike is _____.

c) This is Gavin's book. This book is _____.

d) That is Mr and Mrs Thomson's car. That car is _____.

2 Choose the correct word to complete the sentences.
   Underline the possessive pronouns.

a) That is my parcel.
   That parcel is_____.   (mine/theirs)

b) That is your book.
   The book is _____.   (ours/yours)

c) Those are Lola's sweets.
   Those sweets are _____.   (mine/hers)

d) That is our classroom.
   The classroom is_____.   (ours/his)

e) Those are Bill's, Ted's and Adi's toys.
   The toys are _____.   (his/theirs)

Now try this

Change the underlined words to possessive pronouns.

1 The car is <u>Jenny's</u>. ➡ hers

2 The car is <u>Jack's</u>.

3 The car is <u>Mr and Mrs Patek's</u>.

The suffixes -cian, -sion, -ssion and -tion

Focus

How do you spell words with *-cian*, *-tion*, *-ssion* and *-sion*?

> **Rule**
>
> The suffixes *-cian*, *-tion* and *-ssion* can make the sound *shun* at the end of words.
> The suffix *-sion* can make the sound *zjun*.
>
> The suffix *-tion* is the most common ending.
> **fiction**
>
> The suffix *-cian* is often used for jobs.
> **musician**
>
> The suffix *-sion* is used when the root word ends in *-de* or *-se*.
> **explode → explosion**
> **confuse → confusion**

Practice

1 Add *-cian* to make these into jobs.

   a) politi<u>cian</u>   b) beauti_____   c) techni_____

2 Write the words.

   a)

   b)

   c)

   o_____   e_____   m_____

More to think about

Use the correct box to complete the words.
Use the clues to help you.

| -ation | -ition | -otion | -ution |

1 a liquid that you put on your skin to
   protect or soften it   lotion_____

2 learning and teaching   educ_____

3 something that happens again   repet_____

4 any substance that contaminates air,
   water or land   poll_____

5 the layer of concrete on which a building
   is constructed   found_____

6 an event to find who is best at something   compet_____

7 movement   m_____

8 a complete turn of 360°   revol_____

Now try this

Rewrite the newspaper report, choosing the correct spellings.

There was much panic and (confusion/confussion) today
after a (collission/collision) between a tanker and a lorry.
An (explosion/explossion) was heard shortly after the crash.
Many people were injured and the driver of the tanker was
given a blood (transfusion/transfussion) at the scene of the
accident. When the police are in (possesion/possession) of
all the facts a (discusion/discussion) will take place.

Syllables

Focus

How can dividing a word into syllables help with spelling?

Rule Most words are divided into syllables. Some syllables have vowels that are hard to hear. These are called unstressed vowels.

di/n(o)/saur   o/p(e)n/ing

└──── unstressed ────┘

Pronouncing each syllable slowly and in an exaggerated way can help with spelling.

Practice

Divide these words into syllables and complete the table.

Word	Syllables	Number of syllables
computer	com/put/er	3
desperate		
separate		
hospital		
forgotten		
adventure		
difficult		
roundabout		
general		

More to think about

In the word *demonstrate* the syllables are dem/on/strate.
When you say the word aloud, the unstressed vowel is *o*.
Write the three-syllable words below. Circle the unstressed
vowel each time.

1 din(o)saur

2 o_____

3 e_____

4 b_____

5 f_____

6 a_____

7 a_____

8 m_____

9 e_____

Now try this

Add suffixes to turn these two-syllable
words into three-syllable words.

1 visit<u>or</u>

2 equip_____

3 comfort_____

4 forget_____

5 open_____

6 power_____

7 subtract_____

8 record_____

9 owner_____

10 willing_____

11 employ_____

12 neighbour_____

Common suffixes

Focus

What happens when you add suffixes like -*ed* or -*less* to a word?

Rule If the word ends in *e*, drop the *e* before adding a vowel suffix such as -*ed* or -*ing*.

hope → hoped → hoping

Keep the *e* when adding a consonant suffix such as -*less*.
care → careless

If the word ends in -*y*, change the *y* to *i* when adding a suffix such as -*ness*.
happy → happiness

But do not change the *y* to *i* when adding -*ing*.
play → playing
hurry → hurrying

Practice

1 Add the suffix to the root word.

a) live + ed = lived   b) shame + less   c) pretty + er

d) carry + ing   e) windy + est   f) tune + ing

g) use + ful   h) spite + ful   i) supply + ing

2 Write the root word and the suffix.

a) skating = skate + ing   b) later   c) exciting

d) cheekiest   e) tireless   f) copied

More to think about

Use all the suffixes to make new words.

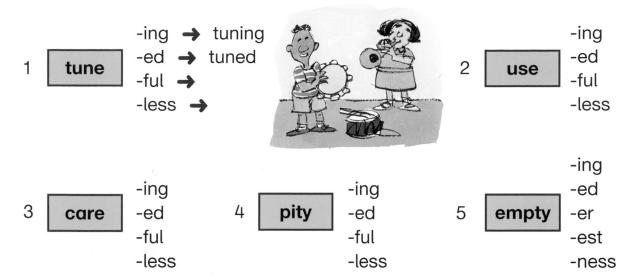

1 **tune**
-ing ➡ tuning
-ed ➡ tuned
-ful ➡
-less ➡

2 **use**
-ing
-ed
-ful
-less

3 **care**
-ing
-ed
-ful
-less

4 **pity**
-ing
-ed
-ful
-less

5 **empty**
-ing
-ed
-er
-est
-ness

Now try this

Some words in the signs have been spelled wrongly.
Write the signs correctly.

1 **Fish and Chips** Friing Tonight

2 Rice supplied with all dishes

5 **Home bakeing**

3 **Horse Rideing** 2 p.m. to 4 p.m.

4 Livly ★music★ every night

8 **Uneven pavments**

6 Photocoping done here

7 The funnyest, sillyest show in town!

Using ie and ei 1

Focus

How do you know whether to spell a word with *ie* or *ei*, like *piece* or *receive*?

 Rule In most words *i* comes before *e*.
piece

But after *c*, *e* comes before *i*.
receive

So remember: *i* before *e* except after *c*.

Practice

1 The letters *ie* can make a long *i* sound, as in **tie**.
Write three words that rhyme with *tie*.

tie: a) ___ie   b) ___ie   c) ___ie

2 The letters *ie* can also make a long *e* sound, as in *piece*.
Write the words.

a)    b)    c)

3 The letters *ier* can also sound like *ear*, as in **tier**.
Write the words.

a) p_____   b) f_____ce   c) p_____ce

More to think about

Copy and complete the table using the words in the box.

piece	pierce	pie	field
niece	tier	brief	cried
pier	tried	tie	lie
dried	fierce	priest	thief

Long *e* sound	Long *i* sound	Sounds like *ear*
piece	pie	pierce

Now try this

Complete the words with *ei* or *ie*.
Use your dictionary to check the spellings.

1 shr_ie_k

2 f____ld

3 n____ce

4 rec____ve

5 conc____ted

6 dec____t

7 rec____pt

8 rel____f

9 bel____ve

10 c____ling

11 gr____f

12 conc____t

Using ie and ei 2

Focus

How do you know whether to spell a word with *ie* or *ei*, like *chief*, *receive* or *weigh*?

Rule

In most words *i* comes before *e*...
chief
...except after *c*.
receive

However, sometimes *ei* can sound like *ai*.
Use *ei* when *ei* sounds like *ai*.
weigh

Use *ei* after *c* when *ei* sounds like *ee*.
ceiling

Practice

Sort the words into two columns.

sleigh	vein	freight	receipt	reign
veil	neighbour	deceive	perceive	weight
rein	deceit	receive	conceit	conceive

ei sounds like *ee*	*ei* sounds like *ai*
receipt	sleigh

More to think about

1 Write these numbers in words.

8   80⅛   88   18

2 Find a homophone that contains the
letters *ei* for each of these words.

a) rain   b) way   c) slay

d) wait   e) vain   f) there

3 Choose two pairs of homophones from question 2.
Write a sentence for each word.

Now try this

1 Add *-ceive* to each prefix to make three more words.
For example:

de + ceive = deceive

| de- | re- | con- | per- |

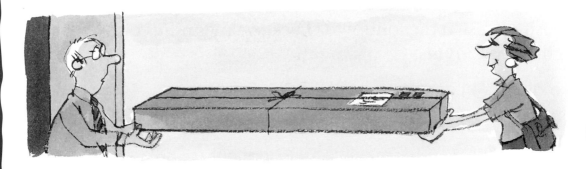

2 Check the meaning of each word in your dictionary.
Use each word in a sentence.

The prefixes il-, im-, ir- and in-

Focus

Let's look at the prefixes *il-*, *im-*, *ir-* and *in-*.

 Rule

The prefixes *il-*, *im-*, *ir-* and *in-* all mean "not".

The prefix *il-* is usually added to words beginning with *l*.
illegal

The prefix *im-* is usually added to words beginning with *m* and *p*.
immobile   **im**patient

The prefix *ir-* is usually added to words beginning with *r*.
irregular

The prefix *in-* is added to most other words.
indefinite

Practice

Add the prefix *im-* to the words below to make their antonyms (opposites). Use a dictionary to check the meanings of the words and their antonyms.

1 mature ➔ immature

2 migrate

3 mobile

4 moral

5 mortal

6 patient

7 perfect

8 possible

9 practical

10 probable

11 moveable

12 partial

More to think about

1 Add the prefix *in-* to the words below.

   a) complete ➜ incomplete   b) accurate   c) audible

   d) adequate   e) capable   f) considerable

   g) flammable   h) formal   i) secure

   j) significant   k) human   l) justice

2 Choose a pair of words from question 1,
  for example:

   complete/incomplete

   Use both words in one sentence. Now choose two more pairs
   of words and do the same for them.

Now try this

Add *ir-* or *il-* to the words below to make new words.

1 legible ➜ illegible   2 regular   3 legal

4 rational   5 logical   6 reversible

7 literate   8 responsible   9 relevant

Progress test 3

A Write the words. They all end in *-ion*.

1

i_____

2

f_____

3

p_____

4

d_____

5

l_____

6

c_____

B Divide the words into syllables and complete the table. Circle the unstressed vowel.

Word	Syllables
motorist	
desperate	
factory	
deafening	
interest	
definite	

46

C Write the words.

1
_____

2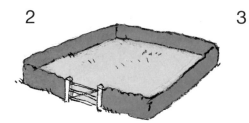
_____

3
_____

4
_____

5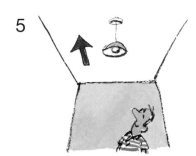
_____

6
_____

D Add the correct prefix to each word below to make a new word.

| im- | ir- | il- | in- |

1 ___resistible

2 ___literate

3 ___perfect

4 ___convenient

5 ___correct

6 ___regular

7 ___practical

8 ___legal

9 ___polite

Well done – you've finished your progress test.

Spellchecker

Write the signs correctly. Then check the spellings in your dictionary.

1 **Bisycle lane**

2 **Sinema Tikkets**

3

Optision

Grate offer!

By won pear, get another pear

free!

4 **Breakfast Serial**

75p

6 Lunchs served daily

Baked potatos
Pizzaes
Fruit salad
 - mangos
 - pairs
 - pineapples
Filled rolles

5 Wieght training at your local jym

 Well done – you've finished your Spellchecker.